SPONSORSHIP PAGE

THIS BOOK IS SPONSORED BY

....

....

AS A GIFT TO

....

....

ON THIS DAY

....

'Each one must give as he has decided in his heart,
not reluctantly or under compulsion,
for God loves a cheerful giver.'
(2 Corinthians 9:7, ESV)

BY PRAYER M. MADUEKE

PRAYERS TO PRAY DURING COURTSHIP

BOOK 7 OF 40 PRAYER GIANTS

FREE EBOOKS

In order to say a 'Thank You' for purchasing *Prayers to Pray during Courtship*, I offer these books to you in appreciation.

> [Click here](https://madueke.com/free-gift) or go to madueke.com/free-gift to download the eBooks now <

MESSAGE FROM THE AUTHOR

PRAYER M. MADUEKE
CHRISTIAN AUTHOR

My name is Prayer Madueke, a spiritual warrior in the Lord's vineyard, an accomplished author, speaker, and expert on spiritual warfare and deliverance. I have published well over 100 books on every area of successful Christian living. I am an acclaimed family and relationship counselor with several titles dealing with critical areas in the lives of the children of God. I travel to several countries each year speaking and conducting deliverance sessions, breaking the yokes of demonic oppression and setting captives free.

It would be a delight to collaborate with you or your ministry in organized crusades, ceremonies, marriages and marriage seminars, special events, church ministration and fellowship for the advancement of God's kingdom here on earth.

You can find all my books on my website: madueke.com.

They have produced many testimonies and I want your testimony to be one too. God bless you.

CHRISTIAN COUNSELLING

We were created for a greater purpose than only survival and God wants us to live a full life.

If you need prayer or counselling, or if you have any other inquiries, please visit the counselling page on my website madueke.com/counselling to know when I will be available for a phone call.

EMAIL NEWSLETTER & ANNOUNCEMENTS

Never miss a message from me again! People who read my newsletters say that they have been one of the most important tools in their Christian walk. The best part is that a subscription is, and always will be, completely free. As a subscriber on my mailing list, you'll be the first to hear about my new book releases, be invited to my weekly prayer sessions, and get reminders about my blog posts and other helpful information.

To subscribe, please visit the newsletter page on my website madueke.com/newsletter.

DEDICATION

This book is dedicated to people who are trusting God to guide them through the period of courtship. The Lord who sees your sincere dedication will answer your prayers Amen.

TABLE OF CONTENTS

ONE

TIME FOR COURTSHIP

Courtship is a period during which couples develop a romantic relationship, especially with a view to marriage. In other words, courtship is a process that leads a man and a woman to marriage. During this time, intending couples come together to know each other well. They find out if they are compatible, and as well find out God's plan for them. It is a time to check if the love they claim to have would stand the test of time without offending God or breaking His Word. If they involve and honor God truly, He would sustain their love for each other.

A friend loveth at all times, and a brother is born for adversity.

— PROVERBS 17:17

Two are better than one; because they have a good reward for their labor. For if they fall, the one will lift up his fellow: but woe to him that is alone when he falleth; for he hath not another to help him up.

— ECCLESIASTES 4:9-10

And Hiram king of Tyre sent his servants unto Solomon; for he had heard that they had anointed him king in the room of his father: for Hiram was ever a lover of David.

— 1 KINGS 5:1

I had no rest in my spirit, because I found not Titus my brother: but taking my leave of them, I went from thence into Macedonia.

— 2 CORINTHIANS 2:13

Henceforth I call you not servants; for the servant knoweth not what his lord doeth: but I have called you friends; for all things that I have

> heard of my Father I have made known unto
> you.
>
> — JOHN 15:15

During courtship, problems and disagreements may arise, but people that make God their bedrock will surely overcome. Godly people disagree in order to agree again. They cannot be weak at the same time. With supernatural strength, they can surmount every challenge. No matter what happens between godly people who are in courtship, there is always solution. This is because God is the source of their love for each other. Because they put God first in everything they do, they will surely stand the test of time.

T W O

PUT GOD FIRST IN YOUR COURTSHIP

In every Christian courtship, the love for God supersedes every other love including the love the man has for the woman and vice versa. However, when the love the man has for the woman or vice versa surpasses the love they have for God, devil takes advantage and enthrones himself in their relationship while pushing God aside. That is why it is important that Christians in courtship engage in discussions, plans and other things that are pure and of good conscience.

> Now the end of the commandment is charity
> out of a pure heart, and of a good conscience,
> and of faith unfeigned... Now unto the King
> eternal, immortal, invisible, the only wise God,
> be honor and glory forever and ever. Amen. This

charge I commit unto thee, son Timothy, according to the prophecies which went before on thee, that thou by them mightest war a good warfare; Holding faith, and a good conscience; which some having put away concerning faith have made shipwreck.

— 1 TIMOTHY 1:5, 17-19

Christians in courtship must realize their need to uphold and honor their relationship with God in their quest to get married. They must not put away their faith in Christ in order to satisfy their carnal desires.

But thou, O man of God, flee these things; and follow after righteousness, godliness, faith, love, patience, meekness. Fight the good fight of faith, lay hold on eternal life, where unto thou art also called, and hast professed a good profession before many witnesses. I give thee charge in the sight of God, who quickeneth all things, and before Christ Jesus, who before Pontius Pilate witnessed a good confession; That thou keep this commandment without spot, unrebukeable, until the appearing of our

Lord Jesus Christ… O Timothy, keep that which
is committed to thy trust, avoiding profane and
vain babblings, and oppositions of science
falsely so called: Which some professing have
erred concerning the faith. Grace be with thee.
Amen. The first to Timothy was written from
Laodicea, which is the chiefest city of Phrygia
Pacatiana.

— 1 TIMOTHY 6:11-14, 20-21

Courtship is not a time to satisfy your carnal lusts. Rather, it is a time to flee from anything that displeased God in order to pursue righteousness, faith, godliness, etc. Therefore, when you lose your faith during courtship, the devil earns a place in the real marriage. However, when you maintain a genuine love for God during your courtship, God would be glorified in your marriage. If you have true love, you would fear God that you would not want to break His law during courtship.

Love worketh no ill to his neighbor: therefore,
love is the fulfilling of the law.

— ROMANS 13:10

> Whether therefore ye eat, or drink, or
> whatsoever ye do, do all to the glory of God.
>
> — 1 CORINTHIANS 10:31

> He that is soon angry dealeth foolishly: and a
> man of wicked devices is hated.
>
> — PROVERBS 14:17

During courtship, most people determine in their hearts to have carnal relationship with their partner at all cost. Unwise people in courtship put pressures on themselves to have sex. Usually, turning down such pressure gets such unwise people angry. Nevertheless, it is better for you to break such relationship at that point than to compromise and live the rest of your life in regrets.

So many problems in most families today are results of selling their birthrights to devil in the name of love. Having sex during courtship gives birth to innumerable problems in marriages. Divine love of God that is enjoyed in marriages disappears whenever people in courtship have sex before their marriage. It is necessary to get together and plan, or even travel together during courtship. However, whenever you do so, do them to the glory of God.

It would be foolish to do something that could only give you satisfaction for a short period during courtship and then keep you in sorrow for the rest of your life. The devil knows how to encourage you to fall out of grace, but you have to resist him. You must consider God in every action you take during your courtship. Courtship is the foundation or pillar that holds every marriage. Therefore, if the foundation is weak, the marriage itself would have problems. Nevertheless, many people fail during the courtship stage.

For other foundation can no man lay than that is laid, which is Jesus Christ. Now if any man build upon this foundation gold, silver, precious stones, wood, hay, stubble; Every man's work shall be made manifest: for the day shall declare it, because it shall be revealed by fire; and the fire shall try every man's work of what sort it is. If any man's work abide which he hath built thereupon, he shall receive a reward. If any man's work shall be burned, he shall suffer loss: but he himself shall be saved; yet so as by fire.

— 1 CORINTHIANS 3:11-15

Some actions you take during courtship are capable of introducing serpent, strange fires and other evil forces into the foundation of your marriage. When you give devil a place in your courtship, he comes in with all manner of problems. In most cases, devil makes a woman to hate the husband and love other men outside her home. At other times, he causes the love the man had for his wife to expire just at the point of their real marriage. For some people, their love may last for a while before it finally expires. That is why many families are suffering today.

Most couples live together physically but spiritually they are divorced. Devil could get at such couples through criticism, lack of affection, failure to leave and cleave, abdication of duties, childlessness and other problems, which lead most people into polygamy or separation. Many married people who claimed to be Christians are having many problems today because they refused to deal with their past.

Strange wives and husbands torment others in their dreams. Others have separated, remarried and yet there is no peace in sight. Some have succeeded in their careers but remained empty in their marital lives. Others face divorce threats, terrible marriage instabilities, frustrations, rebellious children and waste of health. They experience difficulties, lusts for other men or women. The list is endless.

Victims of troubled marriages experience denial of sex from their partners, feigned love from their partners, barrenness and mysterious miscarriages, or consistent complications during delivery. I want to tell you this truth today; sins you committed during courtship could be the reason for reoccurring failures and problems you face in your marriage. In addition, inadequate repentance has made it impossible for many to receive deliverance from God. Therefore, today is another day of grace. Repent and be saved.

> And Samuel spake unto all the house of Israel, saying, If ye do return unto the LORD with all your hearts, then put away the strange gods and Ashtaroth from among you, and prepare your hearts unto the LORD, and serve him only: and he will deliver you out of the hand of the Philistines. Then the children of Israel did put away Baalim and Ashtaroth, and served the LORD only.
>
> — 1 SAMUEL 7:3-4

If people could repent truthfully and faithfully, deliverance would be easy. Instead of blaming God, blame yourself. It is not possible for God to make mistakes. Examine your past and amend your ways. Do not allow your past to destroy your present and future.

THREE

UNPROFITABLE COURTSHIP

When you ignore God and reject His counsels during your courtship, He cannot attend your wedding no matter the amount or quality of crowd you are able to attract on your wedding day.

Because I have called, and ye refused; I have stretched out my hand, and no man regarded; But ye have set at nought all my counsel, and would none of my reproof: I also will laugh at your calamity; I will mock when your fear cometh; When your fear cometh as desolation, and your destruction cometh as a whirlwind; when distress and anguish cometh upon you. Then shall they call upon me, but I will not answer; they shall seek me early, but they shall not find me: For that they hated knowledge, and did not choose the fear of the LORD: They would none of my counsel: they despised all my reproof. Therefore, shall they eat of the fruit of their own way, and be filled with their own devices. For the turning away of the simple shall slay them, and the prosperity of fools shall destroy them.

— PROVERBS 1:24-32

The most important time to bring God into your marriage is during your courtship. Once you allow God to lay the foundation of your marriage, you have achieved a lot already. When God builds the foundation of your marriage during your courtship, no power can overcome your marriage.

Therefore whosoever heareth these sayings of mine, and doeth them, I will liken him unto a wise man, which built his house upon a rock: And the rain descended, and the floods came, and the winds blew, and beat upon that house; and it fell not: for it was founded upon a rock. And every one that heareth these sayings of mine, and doeth them not, shall be likened unto a foolish man, which built his house upon the sand: And the rain descended, and the floods came, and the winds blew, and beat upon that house; and it fell: and great was the fall of it.

— MATTHEW 7: 24-27

A wise builder takes time to build. A wise builder builds with good materials and at the right place. A good builder builds upon the rock.

And it came to pass afterward, that he loved a woman in the valley of Sorek, whose name was Delilah. And the lords of the Philistines came up unto her, and said unto her, Entice him, and see wherein his great strength lieth, and by what means we may prevail against him, that we may bind him to afflict him: and we will give thee every one of us eleven hundred pieces of silver. And she made him sleep upon her knees; and she called for a man, and she caused him to shave off the seven locks of his head; and she began to afflict him, and his strength went from him. And she said, The Philistines be upon thee,

Samson. And he awoke out of his sleep, and said, I will go out as at other times before, and shake myself. And he wist not that the LORD was departed from him.

— JUDGES 16:4-5, 19-20

For she hath cast down many wounded: yea, many strong men have been slain by her. Her house is the way to hell, going down to the chambers of death.

— PROVERBS 7:26- 27

When you give God His rightful place from the beginning of the relationship, He determines the right path for the marriage to His glory. The reason many Christians fail in marriage today is that they do not learn enough about marriage before going into it. Thus, inevitable challenges that take place in marriage take them unawares.

Now the priest of Midian had seven daughters: and they came and drew water, and filled the troughs to water their father's flock. And the shepherds came and drove them away: but

Moses stood up and helped them, and watered their flock. And when they came to Reuel their father, he said, how is it that ye are come so soon to day? And they said, An Egyptian delivered us out of the hand of the shepherds, and also drew water enough for us, and watered the flock. And he said unto his daughters, And, where is he? Why is it that ye have left the man? Call him, that he may eat bread. And Moses was content to dwell with the man: and he gave Moses Zipporah his daughter.

— EXODUS 2:16-21

And it came to pass by the way in the inn, that the LORD met him, and sought to kill him. Then Zipporah took a sharp stone, and cut off the foreskin of her son, and cast it at his feet, and said, Surely a bloody husband art thou to me. So, he let him go: then she said, A bloody husband thou art, because of the circumcision.

— EXODUS 4: 24-26

Unpreparedness and God's absence are able to kill the joy, peace and rest of any marriage. People who think they are very experienced and knowledgeable are often ignorant about marriage and how it works. In the case of Solomon, women messed him up with all his wisdom through his ludicrous marriages.

> But king Solomon loved many strange women, together with the daughter of Pharaoh, women of the Moabites, Ammonites, Edomites, Zidonians, and Hittites; Of the nations concerning which the LORD said unto the children of Israel, Ye shall not go in to them, neither shall they come in unto you: for surely they will turn away your heart after their gods: Solomon clave unto these in love. And he had seven hundred wives, princesses, and three hundred concubines: and his wives turned away his heart.
>
> — 1 KINGS 11:1-3

> Moreover, the Nethinims dwelt in Ophel, unto the place over against the water gate toward the east, and the tower that lieth out.
>
> — NEHEMIAH 3:26

The truth is, if Solomon, with all his wisdom, could fail in marriage, then we all need God in our relationships. You must ensure that you invite God in your courtship. Most problems in the world today have their roots in failed marriages and families. The absence of God in our courtships, marriages and families reflect in our nations.

> For which of you, intending to build a tower, sitteth not down first, and counteth the cost, whether he have sufficient to finish it? Lest haply, after he hath laid the foundation, and is not able to finish it, all that behold it begin to mock him, Saying, this man began to build, and was not able to finish.
>
> — LUKE 14:28-30

Marriage is not something one must rush into. It is not an opportunity to satisfy the flesh and despise God's Word. People who are intending to marry must sit down to think and plan how to lay the foundation of their marriage. It is good to know your partner very well. It is wrong to disobey God's Word because you want to please your partner. While it is good to start a relationship, enter into courtship and plan for your marriage, if God is not involved in your plans, you will not receive His blessing.

The foundation of so many marriages today is unclean. That is why devil is mocking these marriages. The reason we hear of so much troubles in many families today is that unwise couples despise the presence of God in their families. Therefore, strive to live a matured Christian life in your courtship. You need to discipline yourself. Nurture good temperament. Cultivate the spirit of self-denial and selflessness. If you want to enjoy a good Christian marriage, it has to be on God's terms.

> Thus, saith the LORD, stand ye in the ways, and see, and ask for the old paths, where is the good way, and walk therein, and ye shall find rest for your souls. But they said, we will not walk therein.
>
> — JEREMIAH 6:16

As a Christian, you must conduct your marriage in a Christian way.

> Know ye not that they which run in a race run all, but one receiveth the prize? So run, that ye

may obtain. And every man that striveth for the mastery is temperate in all things. Now they do it to obtain a corruptible crown; but we an incorruptible. I therefore so run, not as uncertainly; so fight I, not as one that beateth the air: But I keep under my body, and bring it into subjection: lest that by any means, when I have preached to others, I myself should be a castaway.

— 1 CORINTHIANS 9:24-27

One of the reasons many people are not enjoying their marriages now is because of what they did during courtship. You must let God into your courtship in order to have a fruitful marriage. With purity of heart, you must wait patiently until the right time. Through prayers, trust God faithfully until the marriage celebration.

FOUR

PROFITABLE COURTSHIP

As a true Christian, insist on getting married in a right way and with the right person. You must remain prayerful and watchful during courtship. Do not enter into marriage because you want to solve a present problem or because you want to change your present environment and escape a perceived bondage. If those were your basic reasons for getting married, then eventually, you would discover new set of problems, which may be worse than the ones you were avoiding.

Also, do not marry because of pressures from yourself or from others. Sex and intimate physical pleasures or gratification should not also be the purpose you want to marry. You need to encounter God's love bestowed on your heart and the heart of your partner. Do not marry because of temporary need or attraction. These things are limited.

Set me as a seal upon thine heart, as a seal upon thine arm: for love is strong as death; jealousy is cruel as the grave: the coals thereof are coals of fire, which hath a most vehement flame. Many waters cannot quench love, neither can the floods drown it: if a man would give all the substance of his house for love, it would utterly be contemned.

— SONG OF SOLOMON 8:6-7

I am come into my garden, my sister, my spouse: I have gathered my myrrh with my spice; I have eaten my honeycomb with my honey; I have drunk my wine with my milk: eat, O friends; drink, yea, drink abundantly, O beloved.

— SONG OF SOLOMON 5:1

Who is this that cometh out of the wilderness
like pillars of smoke, perfumed with myrrh and
frankincense, with all powders of the merchant?
Behold his bed, which is Solomon's; threescore
valiant men are about it, of the valiant of Israel.

— SONG OF SOLOMON 3:6-7

Allow the Spirit of God to lead you. Determine to honor God's purpose in your life with eternity in view. Your right partner will go to any length to marry you when you show your determination to do God's will, which He revealed to you.

Not with eye service, as men pleasers; but as
the servants of Christ, doing the will of God
from the heart; With good will doing service, as
to the Lord, and not to men: Knowing that
whatsoever good thing any man doeth, the
same shall he receive of the Lord, whether he be
bond or free.

— EPHESIANS 6:6-8

Your right partner may disagree with you or abandon you for a while but God has a way of bringing him or her back to you when He sees your sincerity in doing His will and determination to fulfill His purpose for your life. When you trust God in faith, God would answer your prayers.

> Shadrach, Meshach, and Abed-nego, answered and said to the king, O Nebuchadnezzar, we are not careful to answer thee in this matter. If it be so, our God whom we serve is able to deliver us from the burning fiery furnace, and he will deliver us out of thine hand, O king. But if not, be it known unto thee, O king, that we will not serve thy gods, nor worship the golden image which thou hast set up.

> — DANIEL 3:16-18

You must be determined to abandon popular worldviews of getting married and look through the eyes of the Spirit. The Spirit is able to provide the leadership that you need.

> Can two walk together, except they be agreed?.

> — AMOS 3:3

Thou shalt not plow with an ox and an ass together.

— DEUTERONOMY 22:10

Let your decision be based on your findings as led by the Holy Spirit. You may listen to a prophecy or an elder's counsel, but you have to prove and test them.

I have not sent these prophets, yet they ran: I have not spoken to them, yet they prophesied. But if they had stood in my counsel, and had caused my people to hear my words, then they should have turned them from their evil way, and from the evil of their doings. Am I a God at hand, saith the LORD, and not a God afar off? Can any hide himself in secret places that I shall not see him? Saith the LORD. Do not I fill heaven and earth? Saith the LORD. I have heard what the prophets said, that prophesy lies in my name, saying, I have dreamed, I have dreamed. How long shall this be in the heart of the prophets that prophesy lies? Yea, they are prophets of the deceit of their own heart; Which think to cause my people to forget my name by their dreams which they tell every man to his neighbor, as their fathers have forgotten my name for Baal. The prophet that hath a dream, let him tell a dream; and he that hath my word, let him speak my word faithfully. What is the chaff to the wheat? Saith the LORD. Is not my word like as a fire? Saith the LORD; and like a hammer that breaketh the rock in pieces? Therefore, behold, I am against the prophets, saith the LORD, that steal my words everyone from his neighbor. Behold, I am against the prophets, saith the LORD, that use their tongues, and say, He saith. Behold, I am against them that prophesy false dreams, saith the LORD, and do tell them, and cause my people to err by their lies, and by their lightness; yet I sent them not, nor commanded them: therefore they shall not profit this people at all, saith the LORD.

— JEREMIAH 23:21-32

For he that speaketh in an unknown tongue speaketh not unto men, but unto God: for no man understandeth him; howbeit in the spirit he speaketh mysteries.

—   1 CORINTHIANS 14:2

Beloved, believe not every spirit, but try the spirits whether they are of God: because many false prophets are gone out into the world. Hereby know ye the Spirit of God: Every spirit that confesseth that Jesus Christ is come in the flesh is of God: And every spirit that confesseth not that Jesus Christ is come in the flesh is not of God: and this is that spirit of antichrist, whereof ye have heard that it should come; and even now already is it in the world. Ye are of God, little children, and have overcome them: because greater is he that is in you, than he that is in the world. They are of the world: therefore, speak they of the world, and the world heareth them. We are of God: he that knoweth God heareth us; he that is not of God heareth not us. Hereby know we the spirit of truth, and the spirit of error.

—   1 JOHN 4:1-6

Be mindful that many false prophets have deceived many people with their wrong teachings concerning marriage. Scrutinize every prophecy by the Spirit of God that is in you so that you do not fail prey to false prophesy. Your decision is the one that matters. Make sure that you and your partner are spiritually compatible. Intellectual and physical compatibility are good but not enough. You need spiritual compatibility also. Utilize the time of your courtship wisely. It is the only time to study and know each other. It is a time of preparation and discussions about the future. It is a time to share your goals in life and things that would affect your family.

Let us therefore follow after the things which make for peace, and things wherewith one may edify another. For meat destroy not the work of God. All things indeed are pure; but it is evil for that man who eateth with offence. It is good neither to eat flesh, nor to drink wine, nor anything whereby thy brother stumbleth, or is offended, or is made weak. Hast thou faith? Have it to thyself before God. Happy is he that condemneth not himself in that thing which he alloweth. And he that doubteth is damned if he eat, because he eateth not of faith: for whatsoever is not of faith is sin.

— ROMANS 14:19-23

From the time of courtship to the wedding day, do everything to the glory of God and to the edification of all believers.

29

FIVE

CORRECTING MISTAKES DURING COURTSHIP

The problem with many people in courtship is pride and stubbornness. People know how to pretend to be holy when they are not. God cannot praise anyone for committing sin. When you delay your repentance and continue in your sins, you receive punishment. When you fail to resist the devil, he comes with guilt and condemnation to make you suffer.

> Submit yourselves therefore to God. Resist the devil, and he will flee from you.
>
> — JAMES 4: 7

If we say that we have no sin, we deceive ourselves, and the truth is not in us. If we confess our sins, he is faithful and just to forgive us our sins, and to cleanse us from all unrighteousness. If we say that we have not sinned, we make him a liar, and his word is not in us.

— 1 JOHN 1:8-10

When you commit sin with your partner during your courtship, there is need for both of you to confess your sins and repent of them before going into marriage.

Examine yourselves, whether ye be in the faith; prove your own selves. Know ye not your own selves, how that Jesus Christ is in you, except ye be reprobates?.

— 2 CORINTHIANS 13:5

And Joshua said unto Achan, my son, give, I pray thee, glory to the LORD God of Israel, and make confession unto him; and tell me now what thou hast done; hide it not from me. And Achan answered Joshua, and said, Indeed I

have sinned against the LORD God of Israel,
and thus and thus have I done: When I saw
among the spoils a goodly Babylonish garment,
and two hundred shekels of silver, and a wedge
of gold of fifty shekels weight, then I coveted
them, and took them; and, behold, they are hid
in the earth in the midst of my tent, and the
silver under it. And Joshua said, why hast thou
troubled us? The LORD shall trouble thee this
day. And all Israel stoned him with stones, and
burned them with fire, after they had stoned
them with stones.

— JOSHUA 7:19-21, 25

Do not postpone your repentance until troubles start. Confess your sins at the right time to avoid destruction. Your deliverance cannot be complete without true repentance. True repentance is the turning away from all sins after confession. You must have a change of mind, purpose and character. Godly sorrow helps you to abhor sin with perfect hatred and to reject sin with all your heart.

The men of Nineveh shall rise in judgment with
this generation, and shall condemn it: because

they repented at the preaching of Jonas; and, behold, a greater than Jonas is here.

— MATTHEW 12:41

But let man and beast be covered with sackcloth, and cry mightily unto God: yea, let them turn everyone from his evil way, and from the violence that is in their hands. Who can tell if God will turn and repent, and turn away from his fierce anger that we perish not? And God saw their works, that they turned from their evil way; and God repented of the evil, that he had said that he would do unto them; and he did it not.

— JONAH 3:8-10

Therefore, I will judge you, O house of Israel, every one according to his ways, saith the Lord GOD. Repent, and turn yourselves from all your transgressions; so, iniquity shall not be your ruin.

— EZEKIEL 18:30

It is a dangerous thing to transfer sins of your courtship into your marriage. If you have done so already, you can still repent with all your heart. I also want to tell you that repentance has levels. It must be deep before true deliverance can come. No one can mock God.

> Be not deceived; God is not mocked: for whatsoever a man soweth, that shall he also reap. For he that soweth to his flesh shall of the flesh reap corruption; but he that soweth to the Spirit shall of the Spirit reap life everlasting.
>
> — GALATIANS 6:7-8

True repentance and restitution bring complete and deep deliverance.

> And there was a man of mount Ephraim, whose name was Micah. And he said unto his mother, the eleven hundred shekels of silver that were taken from thee, about which thou cursedst, and spakest of also in mine ears, behold, the silver is with me; I took it. And his mother said, blessed be thou of the LORD, my son.

— JUDGES 17:1-2

Before your marriage, do not pretend to be holy when you are
not.

WARFARE SECTION

PRAYERS TO PRAY DURING COURTSHIP

Bible Reference: <u>Matthew 1:18-25</u>

Begin with praise and worship

End every step with prayers as you led

STEP 1

Let every enemy of my courtship be exposed and disgraced, in the name of Jesus. Any evil power that is standing between my life partner and I, die, in the name of Jesus. Father Lord, reveal to me all that I need to know during this courtship, in the name of Jesus. Let darkness in my courtship be exposed by divine light, in the name of Jesus. I disgrace any power that wants me to offend my God during this courtship, in the name of Jesus. I refuse to fall victim to any painful and heart-breaking mistake that was prepared to destroy my courtship, in the name of Jesus. I receive power to honor God during my courtship, in the name of Jesus. O Lord, empower me for a godly marriage, in the name of Jesus. Any evil plantation that exists in my courtship, die, in the name of Jesus. Let the fire of God burn every problem that has risen in my courtship, in the name of Jesus. Every disagreement that was designed to destroy God's presence in my courtship, be frustrated, in the name of Jesus. O Lord, arise and take charge over my courtship, in the name of Jesus. Every arrow of immorality and sinful characters that was planted in my courtship, backfire, in the name of Jesus.

STEP 2

O Lord, help my partner and I to understand ourselves to Your glory, in the name of Jesus. Let the presence of God characterize the period of my courtship, in the name of Jesus. Every enemy of godliness in my courtship, be disgraced by fire, in the name of Jesus. Any evil seed that was planted to destroy my courtship, die, in the name of Jesus. Every serpent of darkness in the garden of my courtship, die, in the name of Jesus. I destroy witches or wizards that were empowered to destroy my courtship, in the name of Jesus. O Lord, help me to please You in my courtship, in the name of Jesus. O Lord, if this relationship is not from You, terminate it peacefully, in the name of Jesus. Every demonic impossibility that is standing against this courtship, be removed, in the name of Jesus. O Lord, help me to avoid evil actions during this courtship, in the name of Jesus. Any invitation that I have given to devil in this courtship, I withdraw you, in the name of Jesus. Any problem that wants to enter into my marriage from this courtship, die, in the name of Jesus. O Lord, expand our love from this courtship to our marriage, in the name of Jesus.

STEP 3

O Lord, let Your affection increase during this courtship to Your glory, in the name of Jesus. Every enemy of peace in this courtship, be disgraced by fire, in the name of Jesus. Let every hidden problem in this courtship be exposed and disgraced, in the name of Jesus. Any power that has vowed to remove God in this courtship, die, in the name of Jesus. Let the power that terminates joy, love and peace during courtships die for my sake, in the name of Jesus. Every arrow of inherited problem that was fired into my courtship, I fire you back, in the name of Jesus. I Waste any power that wants to stop my marriage through this courtship, in the name of Jesus. Blood of Jesus, speak Your peace into my courtship, in the name of Jesus. Any power that wants to make my courtship unprofitable, die in shame, in the name of Jesus.

STEP 4

I refuse to ignore God and His Word in my courtship, in the name of Jesus. Father Lord, give me Your counsel that will make my courtship profitable, in the name of Jesus. O Lord, arise and build my marriage during this courtship, in the name of Jesus. Every good thing that will make my courtship profitable, appear, in the name of Jesus. Let failure that was prepared against my marriage during courtship collapse, in the name of Jesus. Let any power that has vowed to ruin my joy during my courtship be wasted, in the name of Jesus. I refuse to enter into proper marriage without God's approval, in the name of Jesus. Father Lord, lead me from the beginning until the end of this courtship, in the name of Jesus. Any power that has vowed to divert me to unprofitable courtship, die, in the name of Jesus.

STEP 5

O Lord, forgive me from every sin I committed before and during this courtship, in the name of Jesus. Any evil that wants to live in my courtship, you are a liar, die, in the name of Jesus. Blood of Jesus, speak me out of problems during this courtship, in the name of Jesus. O Lord, if You are not involved fully in this relationship, stop it now, in the name of Jesus. I refuse to postpone my repentance and confession in this relationship, in the name of Jesus. I cut off every problem that wants to see the light on my weeding day, in the name of Jesus. Let the angels of the living God oppose every enemy of my marriage, in the name of Jesus. Let the earth open to swallow every enemy of my courtship and wedding, in the name of Jesus. Father Lord, perfect this courtship and deliver us from errors, in the name of Jesus.

THANK YOU!

I'd like to use this time to thank you for purchasing my books and helping my ministry and work. Any copy of my book you buy helps to fund my ministry and family, as well as offering much-needed inspiration to keep writing. My family and I are very thankful, and we take your assistance very seriously.

You have already accomplished so much, but I would appreciate an honest review of some of my books through the link below. This is critical since reviews reflect how much an author's work is respected.

Please visit https://www.amazon.com/review/create-review?asin=B09TDPT95F or CLICK HERE TO LEAVE A REVIEW

Please be aware that I read and value all comments and reviews. You can always post a review even though you haven't finished the book yet, and then edit your reviews later.

Once again, here is the link:

Please visit https://www.amazon.com/review/create-review?asin=B09TDPT95F or CLICK HERE TO LEAVE A REVIEW

Thank you so much as you spare a precious moment of your time and may God bless you and meet you at the very point of your need.

You can also send me an email to prayermadu@yahoo.com if you encounter any difficulty while writing your review.

OTHER BOOKS BY PRAYER MADUEKE

1. 100 Days Prayers to Wake Up Your Lazarus
2. 15 Deliverance Steps to Everlasting Life
3. 21/40 Nights of Decrees and Your Enemies Will Surrender
4. 35 Deliverance Steps to Everlasting Rest
5. 35 Special Dangerous Decrees
6. 40 Prayer Giants
7. Alone with God
8. Americans, May I Have Your Attention Please
9. Avoid Academic Defeats
10. Because You Are Living Abroad
11. Biafra of My Dream
12. Breaking Evil Yokes
13. Call to Renew Covenant
14. Command the Morning, Day and Night
15. Community Liberation and Solemn Assembly
16. Comprehensive Deliverance
17. Confront and Conquer Your Enemy
18. Contemporary Politicians' Prayers for Nation Building
19. Crossing the Hurdles
20. Dangerous Decrees to Destroy Your Destroyers (Series)
21. Dealing with Institutional Altars
22. Deliverance by Alpha and Omega

FREE EBOOKS

In order to say a 'Thank You' for purchasing *Prayers to Pray during Courtship*, I offer these books to you in appreciation.

> **Click here or go to madueke.com/free-gift to download the eBooks now** <

CHRISTIAN COUNSELLING

We were created for a greater purpose than only survival and God wants us to live a full life.

If you need prayer or counselling, or if you have any other inquiries, please visit the counselling page on my website madueke.com/counselling to know when I will be available for a phone call.

EMAIL NEWSLETTER & ANNOUNCEMENTS

Never miss a message from me again! People who read my newsletters say that they have been one of the most important tools in their Christian walk. The best part is that a subscription is, and always will be, completely free. As a subscriber on my mailing list, you'll be the first to hear about my new book releases, be invited to my weekly prayer sessions, and get reminders about my blog posts and other helpful information.

To subscribe, please visit the newsletter page on my website madueke.com/newsletter.

AN INVITATION TO BECOME A MINISTRY PARTNER

In response to several calls from readers of my books on how to collaborate with this ministry, we are grateful to provide our ministry's bank details.

Be assured that our continued prayers for you will be answered according to God's Word, and as you remain faithful by sowing seeds of faith, God will never forget your labors of love in Christ Jesus.

Send your Seeds to:

In Nigeria & Africa

Bank Name: **Access Bank**

Account Name: **Prayer Emancipation Missions**

Account Number: **0692638220**

In the United States & the rest of the World

Bank Name: **Bank of America**

Account Name: **Roseline C. Madueke**

Account Number: **483079070578**

You can also visit the donation page on my website to donate online: www.madueke.com/donate.